BOA
EDITIONS LTD

THE FORTIETH DAY

The Fortieth Day

Poems by
Kazim Ali

American Poets Continuum Series, No. 110

BOA Editions, Ltd. ∞ Rochester, NY ∞ 2008

First Edition
08 09 10 11   7 6 5 4 3 2 1

For information about permission to reuse any material from this book please contact
The Permissions Company at www.permissionscompany.com or e-mail permdude@
eclipse.net.

Publications and programs by BOA Editions, Ltd.—a not-for-profit corporation under section
501 (c) (3) of the United States Internal Revenue Code—are made possible with the assistance
of grants from the Literature Program of the New York State Council on the Arts; the Lit-
erature Program of the National Endowment for the Arts; the County of Monroe, NY; the
Lannan Foundation for support of the Lannan Translations Selection Series; the Sonia Raiziss
Giop Charitable Foundation; the Mary S. Mulligan Charitable Trust; the Rochester Area
Community Foundation; the Arts & Cultural Council for Greater Rochester; the Steeple-Jack
Fund; the Ames-Amzalak Memorial Trust in memory of Henry Ames, Semon Amzalak and
Dan Amzalak; and contributions from many individuals nationwide. See Colophon on page
80 for special individual acknowledgments.

Cover Design: Lisa Mauro
Cover Art Photograph: Rachel Eliza Griffiths
Interior Design and Composition: Richard Foerster
Manufacturing: Thomson-Shore
BOA Logo: Mirko

Library of Congress Cataloging-in-Publication Data

Ali, Kazim, 1971–
  The fortieth day : poems / by Kazim Ali. — 1st ed.
     p. cm. — (American poets contiuum series ; no. 110)
  Includes bibliographical references.
  ISBN 978–1–934414–04–0 (pbk. : alk. paper)
  I. Title. II. Title: 40th day.
  PS3601.L375F67 2007
  811'.6—dc22

                           2007038074

                      BOA Editions, Ltd.
          Nora A. Jones, Executive Director/Publisher
               Thom Ward, Editor/Production
              Peter Conners, Editor/Marketing
              A. Poulin, Jr., Founder (1938–1996)
            250 North Goodman Street, Suite 306
                   Rochester, NY 14607
                    www.boaeditions.org

NATIONAL
ENDOWMENT
FOR THE ARTS

State of the Arts

NYSCA

Contents

1

2

to Marco Wilkinson

LOSTNESS

dear God of blankness I pray to dear unerasable

how could I live without You if I were ever given answers

the summer thickens with lostness

lovers who will not touch each other but look out into space

thinking I do not belong in the world

news always travels inland but how can this storm

be undone or the treacherous rain unravel or the train

arriving one street over and all night long

on an island at the end of islands a foresworn vow

a river blasted through and another river filled in

dear afternoon God dear evening God my lonely world

the circles of water and wanton violence

dear utterly unmistakable ether

dear Lostness your careless supplicant drops everything

and rakes over me on his way to an implacable place

MORNING PRAYER

the work of dark
a tremulous sound

Mount Beacon season to season
changes or is changed

what's in us that reaches
to know what's after

should I draw the spirit
as a lantern or a cup

DEAR FATHER, DEAR SOUND

I exist only two cosmic minutes after you,
an echo of your life's whispering.

You recited into my ears the call to prayer
before I had either language or sight.

Your whisper and the secret my life whispered in response
are going at the speed of sound to the end of the universe.

Will they ever reach it?
Will they ever begin traveling back?

Dear Sunset, Dear Avalanche

dear thunder without lightning
dear window sound of last year

dear mountainous landscape
unfolding

water in air unraveling
dear ice filled clamor that fetches

I'm fetching, tolling, a libelous suit
sold and soldiering up the slopes

navigating the trails without adequate supplies
opening up the roof of the ride

a somnambulist, a compassless climber,
a lunchless hack, naked on the rock road

my ear cocked to the distance
dear solo slipping sun

this is the part the slow whispering interrupts
dear disappeared, dear desperate

this is the part you're always interrupting,
the part you want to be buried under—

Mouth

When he can't stop re-reading, *were all the trees made into pens*
and all the oceans into ink, with seven more oceans to increase it,
still the words of God would not come to an end,

he thinks, is it possible the entire universe is scrap metal
for meditation or never-ending revelation?

"No," writes his left-handed angel, "you are misreading yet again:

"The soldiers hunting for the hidden prophet on the mountain never
even thought to look in the cave of revelation:

"A spider had spun a web over the mouth immediately following his
passage inside."

The Art of Breathing

Do you lose yourself
in the cave of endless breath,

the moment you don't want to know yourself,
soaring or frightened—

Says Arjuna on the battlefield, throwing down his bow,
"I refuse to fight my cousins and kin."

Replies dark-blue Krishna, "These are only tricks and metaphor,
Your selfishness and separation, your cheapness and rage."

So when Karna's chariot wheel breaks,
and he stumbles down to fix it,

Krishna whips the horses faster towards them. "Shoot!" he yells
to Arjuna, "You can destroy your own alienation if you do it!"

Arjuna pulls his arrow back and looks long through the sight
at his secret brother, the broken wheel—

The Far Mosque

after Rumi

Where is the place to which the prophet flew?

The mosque Sulayman built is not made of minarets or stone—
The muezzin and his voice both live there like lovers.

A person is only a metaphor for the place he wants to go.

Rope

The wintered plot concludes in a chapter he refuses to translate

The lyre is a liar, a string of gut pulled taut

As a newborn his father whispered into his ears the call to prayer

Each strand of his father's voice a shaft of light from Heaven

A rope thrown down to rescue him

He wants to grab hold, climb up, disappear

CAVE

There is a web of blue and green in his dream,
seedlings of sky and grass thrusting up from the ground.

Years after his promise to his body was broken
and the silver cord severed,

the spirit sent like a ghost ship to trawl the dream terrain,
wrinkled and blue—

Music leaks roughly from the body
the way the stomach empties itself of vomit—

Days and days after he stays weak
making the promise, writing it into all the crevices and corners—

One vow could cut through all the surf,
commend him to a steady stream of silver cords—

But isn't it better, his tricky innards reason with him,
to be like this: lost, afraid, hungry and alone,

deafened in the cave of your own breath,
no web spun across the mouth, no angel inside—

Chasm

source-opener, metal-worshipper,
basket-body, garden-limber,

you win this round, I give—
Aztec, Toltec, train-wreck,

why do you not colossus me
how is it you Babylon me

Babel me, sun whisper
and steeple me

rain charm sky bed I wonder
at the dimness of your zero music

this is the chasm of breath
the wound cave

funny how you say I'm in "danger"
because finally I feel not in danger—

all this time I have been speaking
to nothing but wildness

and now wildness is answering—

Vase

He wrote to you once, night's cold I,
storm-broken branches,

here in this room on the galaxy's edge.

He wrote to you twice, sun-yellow dusk,
midnight enameled vase,

snow-blue shelf in the sky.

He wrote to you three times,
and the nothing inside flew up,

a listless prisoner, tethered, a spy.

2

THE YEAR OF WINTER

It has been spilled to me, my parentage,
I am aghast—

For ninety-one days the winter has been piercing me,
ninety-one days the year threading through.

How is it possible I ceased to believe in tongues?
The fallen red rimed by morning's white amendments.

Tuesday's reminders: visit the bank,
check the tires, hit the road...

A four-hour drive to Pennsylvania under
autoscrivening sky—

Who can blame my mistrust when the gray sky
revises its most sacred opinions,

who could ever have believed you, mad heart,
that fog and soot are brethren,

the shape of want and war are identical,
a submerged river, flowing eight hundred feet beneath us—

AFTERNOON PRAYER

God, a curt question or a curtain,
the call to prayer fading away.

May I request evening or more rain?
Doing laundry, getting new tires—

May I invest smartly, catch a later train?
Snow fills the margins, sunset across the river.

As we rush north, everything is pulled back,
God, a day's work, the echoing tracks—

ORNITHOGRAPHY

sunlight alarms the room
tattered by time and the failed window

dust motes taking note of the yellow
as it passes through the glass in bars without breaking

a difficult spill from the blue leading to an idea
the sky is you, the bird was you, the glass was you,

are you still, though all broken—

if you sail out on your boat will the air unroll,
will it open into navigable paths

will you single out the sound that lingers
a bow that shivers along the strings

a transcription of the sight of five hundred wings
dreaming a sudden maze

whose feathered arms are gesturing
through dust's field of vision

when you the boat's wake
when the rudder drifts

the surface is still
is it really still since still reaches back

threads the idea of the boat to the idea of water
chores here are choral

the cords of your work connect you
crouched in the shade, dustpan in hand

if lingering is the wind
if the waves of the sky-road are really wind

water is waves
if the boat sails through mist

will the island coalesce
will you coalesce

of dust and light and broken glass

who has to sweep
who has to patch the empty frame

who is going to fly back
to blue

Double Reed

when dusk says hand it over
what am I supposed to hand over

in printing you have to choose
between portrait or landscape

some evenings even though I am cold
I won't go inside for a jacket

the bulb in the hallway has gone out
or did someone purposely unscrew it

I don't know how to talk to you
also I don't know how to listen

I don't know anything about music except
clarinet is single reed and oboe is double reed

doubled in the night and finally warm
I keep thinking about how I didn't lock the doors

the trees have vanished into dark
but evening is the sound of cars in the road

truancy is my life among the succulents
and my ardent wish that the war years be finished

in sculpture you are not supposed to carve
but carve away

double reed means your mouth isn't even touching the instrument
you are only holding a reed against another reed

THE DESERT

To make darkness possible
you close the shutters

When light streams in
it is harder to see

You're inside arguing about whether
a cloud was once a river

While outside a man stutters,
trying to talk to the cacti

If you could receive only one answer
would you choose to know

what he is choking on
or what he is trying to say

The Ocean Floor

Dreamt of being under a spell
A creature prisoned to the ocean floor

What decades I spell looking up
Through acres of water to surface light

The black ovals of ship hulls passing over
Sound travels so slowly

At the bottom of the ocean
Somehow not drowning

My supposed deafness fishes
From water the sound of an orchestra

In which all the instruments play separately
From one another and out of tune

Sleep Door

a light knocking on the sleep door
like the sound of a rope striking the side of a boat

heard underwater
boats pulling up alongside each other

beneath the surface we rub up against each other
will we capsize in

the surge and silence
of waking from sleep

you are a lost canoe, navigating by me
I am the star map tonight

all the failed echoes
don't matter

the painted-over murals
don't matter

you can find your way to me
by the faint star-lamp

we are a fleet now
our prows zeroing in

praying in the wind
to spin like haywire compasses

toward whichever direction
will have us

BOTTLE

in the night-cove tossed
savage spirit bottle lost

the stone-year recites itself backwards
under the guise of rain and restlessness

collapsing quickly into the water
sinking out of sight

those words remain barnacled
not for all the diving and searching found

while ten thousand miles from here
in another moon-turned life

the ocean will receive itself
opening its green pages to glass and sand

Horizon

It's unbearable what you remember;
numb in the storm wanting an answer.

There's a boat that loves to drink;
you love to be tricked or called names.

At its freezing point wind shatters;
were you faking it or really dying?

Pray you, quicksilver, rush to me quickly,
make me mad, unfasten me from shore.

The night has a name the storm is ashamed of;
send me to the earth's end—I have never seen it.

GARLAND

The *mala* around your wrist is meant
to remind you to go back to the stone-year.

When you were cold, locked out,
cocooned, no one called.

Tone deaf and friendless, you decided:
less collage, more song.

More song meant you got limber,
abandoned the agreed-upon ocean.

You remember it as difficult,
but that part was easy.

If time can unmoor itself and cast off,
so can you—

Interrupted Letter

If upon the conclusion of my rain-scene
you compose a reply

and it's letter by letter leaves on the ground,
a crown of wet leaves, a sinecure, a deciduous warning—

The end of time wasn't like this last go around,
wasn't a lake or a gray morning, an apartment I didn't know,

rumpled sheets, a glass half full of water,
the floor above creaking with the weight of

someone who wears shoes even at home—

No one knows how the mind works.

How are you supposed to remember where you live
in a world contracted to expire—

Rain pouring along the pane.
You promised to respond and still there's nothing—

Quiz

my father's hand	a tune carried around in the skin
the road of devotion	how a sirocco unwraps itself
the surface of water	dear lantern dear cup
three miracles	a spider weaving a web across
when will you come back	the moon split in half
an empty basket	the river rose up and flew apart
wind-tossed pilgrim	in the hills above the place
where	you ask for more time

3

The Second Funeral

We will return in forty days and the seam
of the disturbed ground won't be visible.

Death is a miracle I do not understand,
our life already split in half.

Five women across the street hold hands,
forbidden to enter the burial ground.

In forty days our prayers
will have evaporated into winter wind.

What will then stitch the earth closed?
A thread of five cousins, forbidden to cross

and the sixth who went to them,
warm earth in his hands.

Evening Prayer

To say the earth is not stable
is just another way of saying "I don't know"

or "well, what do you know"

Light is blinding and physics fibs:
that you are being whipped

around the galaxy's center
at 25 million miles a second

is purely ridiculous

But if it happens to be true
that space bends and the universe becomes you

you will not mind

The sound of eternity you've been there
The end of time you've been there

Math

Adamant as the jade in the window
the year carries itself into the new season.

When winter turned to summer
I forgot it all like math,

God in the sky and God in the water
dissolving at the horizon,

or God in the air and in the plant condensing
on the glass, a geometry of frost-rime,

because when we went into the ocean,
the waves were glass-green, the sky pure indigo.

In the room last winter's writing
can still be seen.

Who is that in the space where your
self and your self do not meet?

In the ocean our bodies float together
just a few feet apart.

Flight

The clouds drop below us a hundred one meters,
a carpet of wavelets forgets to unravel,

we're spinning a shadow against the deflowered
historical blue, a tornado bequeathing

denuded arrangements, a hasty departure,
the conference fled, its message disbanded.

What widower bird could remain here against
the explicit commands of destructive rebellion?

The war is eternally on, the unmasking
complaint: though we cannot yet hear the recorder

of ravenous charms we still savor belief as
we fall from the sky with the slightest of prayers—

Two Halves

two halves circle each other
each aching for the other's arms

they're rent in their itching
to hit ground at the speed of sound

the half of you is tone deaf
the other half still sings

one half forgot the other's face
his "collision or collusion with history"

the two lock now one to the other
sink blazingly below the clouds

surrendering the instinct to disfigure
the one's half mad by now, a curse-river

he's parched, strung out, devoured
unable to articulate how the other half felt

falling, shrieking, about to cut the sky in half
as for what they were holding when they fell

sun-spilled, thunderous, sundered
each can only remember

the lonely earth, an only child,
given to the mother who will let go

Ramadan

You wanted to be so hungry, you would break into branches,
and have to choose between the starving month's

nineteenth, twenty-first, and twenty-third evenings.
The liturgy begins to echo itself and why does it matter?

If the ground-water is too scarce one can stretch nets
into the air and harvest the fog.

Hunger opens you to illiteracy,
thirst makes clear the starving pattern,

the thick night is so quiet, the spinning spider pauses,
the angel stops whispering for a moment—

The secret night could already be over,
you will have to listen very carefully—

You are never going to know which night's mouth is sacredly reciting
and which night's recitation is secretly mere wind—

Ursa Major

dear mother in the sky
unbuckle the book

and erase all
the annotations

you could suckle or
suffocate me

how will you find
the little polar star in

the vast sky disowned
from his constellation

blinking at you across
unspeakable distance

THE NINTH PLANET

In the shadow cast by the end of time,
who will believe the earth was not merely a vast plain.

Faith requires laws to seize control,
to assure clay's obedience to gravity and light.

Who wouldn't believe that otherwise we would slingshot into space,
that oceans would pour from the earth's stark edges?

The universe is the most human of individuals:
Lowell never saw the proof of Pluto in his lifetime—

observing an erratic wobble in Neptune's orbit,
he plotted diagrams and equations,

left detailed instructions as to where in the night sky
the last once-wanderer would be found

Dear Lantern, Dear Cup

should You light the way
or should You hold me

dear earthquake in the ground
who is waiting

am I shining into infinite space
or will I be spilled

Pastoral: The Bats

and if it was the wind: from under the bridge
in the dark spaces: we lounged, eating cheese, pistachios

and the undercurrent of dusk: that wind
that the underside of afternoon: would fly

that dark places give evidence: it was an afterthought
the sensation of losing: an antagonism

from the bridge or the boat: the shore
from the shore: the sky's arduous ceiling

an ardor, a mellifluous wish: do you know
what you're seeing: or is it simple wonder

this corporate takeover: an animal undertaking
you're seeing: instinct not anguish

you're seeing: a desire to have not to get
either way, dark reaching: the years are not wind

did not send you here: do not promise or give flight
it is just a question of: or is there no question

you must launch yourself: heathen, crime victim
there's no moment: when it stops

only swirls and swirls: disappearing into evening
launch yourself: do you dare

what's most alarming: you thought you would hear
the echo-locating scream: and you don't

Dear Dangerous, How Do You Explain It

We believed the world would end,
fled now into the alley or the forest.

Among the amber that clots minute by minute
or a ship that sails to show how long time takes to happen

How does one skip a stone on water,
the moment between skips.

A preoccupation with god or history is no occupation.
It happens that every day is synchronous

that I am still right now a little boy or dying.
How do you explain it,

seven o'clock, out of breath and arduous—
Dear unsettled evening, all the cold shadows,

how lucky we were to have lived
in the world—

The Cathedral Tower

a dark climb
the span lined by beasts

came in the rain
when the walls of the citadel sprout demons

two birds huddled in a recess
the doors are locked

one city on top of another
and no trace of ruins

the river splits at this island
rejoins itself

the river of my years

4

NAVAL MISSIVE

Will I ever dare to pray for something real or will I stay at the sill,
looking out, wanting to know who is looking back.

I write letters folded as boats,
dropped into the stream at midnight.

Drifting somewhere between map and maelstrom,
should I ask for my thirst to be quenched or for unquenchable thirst—

Night Prayer

On the fortieth day we return to watch the soul
take reluctant leave of the body,

a clot of tissue receives breath, and in the desert
wandering prophets prepare to return.

On the fortieth night, on the storm-lashed boat,
retching and abandoned to eternal fury of storm,

we finally accept in our hearts that
the ocean will never calm

and we will never again know peace.

August

A jigsaw of nothing but sky
Three pieces next to one another
A clamor, a lull, an official complaint
No map provides for sore spots or depths
Not an ounce of white in sight
You're unlocatable
Three different versions of downpour
A trembling instrument
When the wait was empty
Music came out of the woods
Not what you expected
An empty place and no piece to match
How could you turn into blue
What in the world were you doing
When the picture was shown
You receive no image or instruction
What you seek to fit into will not cease

PACKING

"As all the Heavens were a Bell,
And Being, but an Ear"

Pulling down the paintings from the walls,
the orange one, the blue one.

Who I was when I came here
and who I had thought I would become—

ghost twins in the room,
stapling me to the ground,

bibled to the bareness
and the sound of ringing.

They start unpacking,
returning the paintings to the walls.

I sit back and take a rest while they
discuss which of us the Bell,

and which of us the Ear—

PERISH

What am I frightened of night

Twelve voices that cannot manage harmony

Segovia's technique in which the last two fingers pluck

The chapter that's the heart of Moby Dick

Sounds different in the wild

An utterly different pair of strings

That vibrate on their own

Tashtego drowning in sperm oil

Mathematicians in Egypt make precise calculations

Once sung by a single human voice

To relocate all the temples endangered by the dam's construction

Carried by his friend out of danger and back aboard

Pip

He slips between the pages
into depth

Is this what was written
on the body's blank

Who you're praying to
is perhaps

A castaway: lost in publication,
unfinished

The boats mount their
horizonward search

I do not want to drown or
be lost

In blue smoke, a sound of
oars working

My name being
called

FRAGMENT

...adrift on cloud-terrain,
having forgotten my suitcase

boarded the wrong plane
all the ghost-writing goes away

the cold rain stones
the sky's bleak shelf

trade myself here for
a necklace of acorns or a little tree

second state is awareness
third state is waking dream

echoes of river-bed, ocean floor
drying quickly

spirit-uncle, residue
scotch-bonnet, jesus-lizard

passing through
nothing follows the courses

to argument or what
nothing knows

where we're going
nothing will wonder...

Autobiography

we didn't really speak but
my summer wants to answer

the architecture doesn't matter
this is not my real life

when I am here I want to know
why do I believe what I was taught

a storm is on the way
close all the windows

begin at the earliest hour
is there a self

A Century in the Garden

It is hard not to know my death my nowhere trajectory

What is the difference between entity and eternity

I asked him the long syllableless afternoon

The ache a quench the eighty-ninth question

My disappeared friend a body I used to know

It doesn't need to know my death its dark current

Waiting for the Train

who are you perfect wind

clarinet or oboe

Friday working out a methodology of weather

waiting for the train it pleases me to listen

or to look west

water splashing the pier, a car door slams

breeze goes right into my ears

background noise but to what

that there might be a wood-spider on the back of my neck

I am brief and a river

somehow space and far away

after opening my eyes the afternoon becomes blue

birds a breathtaking conference

life while the noise stills uncertain

uncertain the worrisome adversary

or am I the adversary racing for shore

arrangement of birds or a raiment

arraignment of the river for mouthing off

am I music or motion—

the question on which the wind lectures me all afternoon

SUTURE

He wrote to you once
There was no answer

He wrote to you twice
The horizon dolorously sounded itself out

He wrote to you three times
The night spelled your emptiness "I"

LOVE NOTE

A window from the afternoon seems like evening;
nomad, again the wind's eye is asking to see you,

afternoon's restless discussion scatters,
the years are pulled taut as strings

and it is frightening not to know
what this will sound like at the end.

Night unwraps itself then bliss,
I'm in love with you here,

Sunday night and silence,
you're starless, wonder-filled,

a full realization.
Why wouldn't I thrashing and rapt

imagine you as a cool night, a gift, this amazement,
a promise thrown over the railing,

dark to dark, a pen writing back to me
as it falls against the sky,

this is you, in love with a world you cannot see—
the world that promised to be yours and it was yours

Four O'Clock

An old man with a bag of chocolates, lost on the sidewalk, on his way home from the corner store.

He won't be missed until his granddaughter arrives home from school at four o'clock to an empty house.

A mouthful of chocolates, the recitation of a chapter—tangible and intangible ways of saying: "God" or "come home."

Being borne up over elms and houses by waves of voices reciting saffron chapters written into the streets and sky.

Written onto the sheet that years later will be wrapped over him, around his forehead, folded over his mouth.

Illusion is the sheet and the thing lying under it.

Gone the streets he knows, unwritten the map of how to find him.

Dizzy with all the changing directions. It's a minute before four.

Where did I come from? Which way will I be borne?

NOTES

Mouth: The verse is *Luqman:27* from the Qur'an. In Islamic belief there are angels sitting on each of your shoulders writing your life down. The one on the right shoulder writes all your good deeds and the one of the left writes all your misdeeds.

The Far Mosque: Spun around a couple of lines from Rumi's poem of the same name in *Essential Rumi*, translated by Coleman Barks.

Chasm: For Jennifer Chapis. The phrases "basket-body" and "garden-limber" are hers.

Ornithography: The word *ornithography* is meant as the bird-pattern version of orthography.

Double Reed: For Juliet Patterson.

The Second Funeral: In Islamic tradition, a second commemorative service is held on the fortieth day after death. In some traditions, women are not permitted at graveside. For Saira, Sana, Sakina, Naheed, and Aneesa.

Math: For Sakina Sayeed.

Flight: Written in amphibrachs for Annie Finch.

Two Halves: The short quote is from Susan Howe's book *Articulation of Sound Forms in Time* (reprinted in *Singularities*, Wesleyan University Press).

Packing: The epigraph is from Dickinson's poem that begins "I felt a Funeral..."

Pip: Perhaps this poem could be copied from this book and slipped secretly into the final section of Dan Beachy-Quick's *Spell*, from which Pip has gone missing.

A Century in the Garden: Named after a book of the same title by Stanley Kunitz with Genine Lentine. This poem is for them.

Four O'Clock: For Farrah.

Acknowledgments

Some of these poems, often in earlier versions, first appeared in the following journals and anthologies:

American Poetry Review: "Horizon," "Vase," "Four O'Clock";
Barrow Street: "The Art of Breathing," "Waiting for the Train";
Best American Poetry 2007: "The Art of Breathing";
Boston Review: "Garland";
Dragonfire: "Rope";
Eleven Eleven: "Quiz," "Evening Prayer" (as "Constancy"), "The Cathedral Tower";
COAGH: "The Ninth Planet," "Afternoon Prayer" (as "Curtain");
Guernica: "Double Reed";
Joyful Noise: The Autumn House Anthology of Spiritual Literature: "Ramadan";
jubilat: "Dear Sunset, Dear Avalanche";
Massachusetts Review: "Chasm";
New Orleans Review: "Mouth," "The Desert," "The Far Mosque";
Painted Bride Quarterly: "Cave," "Love Note";
South Asian Review: "Interrupted Letter";
Trikone: "Two Halves."

"Naval Missive" (as "Night Prayer"), "Dear Father, Dear Sound," "The Year of Winter," "Interrupted Letter," "Night Prayer" (as "The Fortieth Night") and "Suture" were published as *River Road*, an electronic chapbook, by *The Drunken Boat* (www.thedrunkenboat.com).

"Morning Prayer," "Afternoon Prayer" and the closing couplet of "Interrupted Letter" were published as a broadside by Kseniya Thomas of Thomas Printers in Carlisle, Pennsylvania.

Audio versions of several of these poems can be found at "From the Fishouse" at www.fishousepoems.org.

Many thanks to Meena Alexander, Alex Auder, Russ Carmony, Julie Carr, Annie Finch, Sarah Gambito, Melissa Hammerle, Fanny Howe, Sondra Loring, Roshi Enkyo O'Hara, Robin Beth Schaer, Craig Thompson, and Richard Zumkhawala-Cook.

For insight and feedback on these poems, thanks to Thom Ward, Paula Bohince, Rob Casper, and Jennifer Chapis.

For their guidance, thanks to Nilofer and Hadi Saeed. To my sisters Farrah and Naheed. To Irma Wilkinson. For their faith and the strength they lent me, to Raz and Asker Saeed.

For all things, to Rukia and Asgher Ali.

To the immortal spirits of Dev Hathaway, Shahnaz Sayeed, and Turiya Alice Coltrane. See you after.

And with boundless gratitude for his teaching and love and light, nine bows to Jonji Provenzano.

About the Author

Kazim Ali has worked as a political organizer, lobbyist, and yoga instructor. He has taught writing and literature at various colleges including The Culinary Institute of America, Monroe Community College, Shippensburg University, New York University, and Parsons School of Design; he currently teaches at Oberlin College and in the University of Southern Maine's Stonecoast MFA Program. Co-founder of Nightboat Books, his poetry and essays appear widely in such journals as *American Poetry Review*, *Boston Review*, *jubilat* and in *Best American Poetry 2007*. His other books include a poetry collection, *The Far Mosque*; a novel, *Quinn's Passage*; and the forthcoming *Bright Felon: Autobiography and Cities*.

BOA Editions, Ltd.
American Poets Continuum Series

Colophon

The Fortieth Day, poems by Kazim Ali, is set in Adobe Jenson,
a digital font designed by Robert Slimbach (1956–) based on
the roman typefaces of Nicolas Jenson (1420–1480)
and the italics of Ludovico degli Arrighi (1475–1527).

The publication of this book is made possible, in part,
by the special support of the following individuals:

Anonymous (2)
Jeanne Marie Beaumont
Alan & Nancy Cameros
Gwen & Gary Conners
Wyn Cooper & Shawna Parker
Susan DeWitt Davie
Peter & Sue Durant
Pete & Bev French
Dane & Judy Gordon
Kip & Debby Hale
Peter & Robin Hursh
Willy & Bob Hursh
X. J. & Dorothy M. Kennedy
Laurie Kutchins
Archie & Pat Kutz
Rosemary & Lewis Lloyd
Boo Poulin
Steven O. Russell & Phyllis Rifkin-Russell
Vicki & Richard Schwartz
Thomas R. Ward
Patricia D. Ward-Baker
Pat & Mike Wilder
Glenn & Helen William